Fricción positiva, fricción negativa
Good Friction, Bad Friction

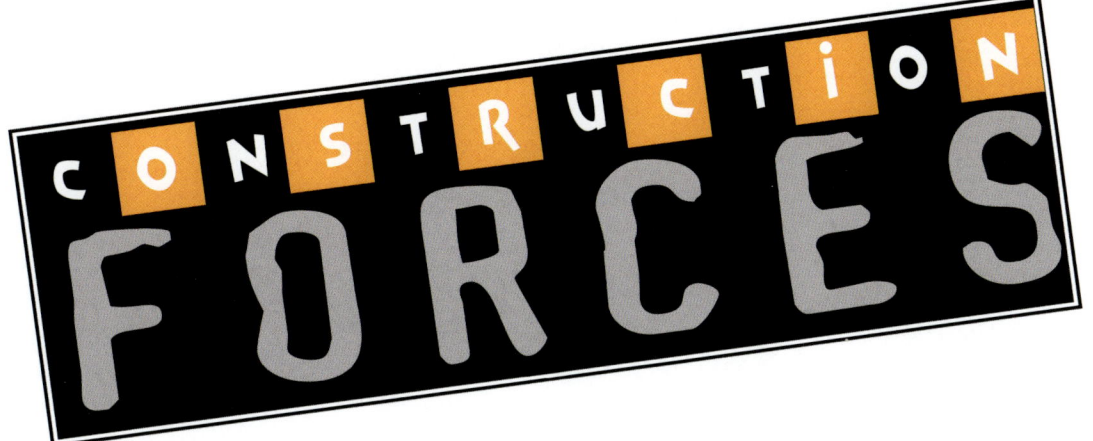

Patty Whitehouse

Vero Beach, Florida 32964

© 2007 Rourke Publishing LLC

All rights reserved. No part of this book may be reproduced or utilized in any form or by any means, electronic or mechanical including photocopying, recording, or by any information storage and retrieval system without permission in writing from the publisher.

www.rourkepublishing.com

PHOTO CREDITS: © David and Patricia Armentrout: pages 4, 6, 7, 9, 14, 15, 19, 22; © Craig Lopetz: pages 5, 8, 12, 20; © PIR: pages 10, 13, 17; © constructionphotographs.com: page 11; © Michael Efford: page 18; © Chris Pollack: page 21

Editor: Robert Stengard-Olliges

Cover and interior design by Nicola Stratford

Library of Congress Cataloging-in-Publication Data

Whitehouse, Patricia, 1958-
 Fricción positiva, fricción negativa (Good friction, bad friction) / Patty Whitehouse.
   p. cm. -- (Fueraza de construccion/Construction forces)
 Includes index.
 ISBN-10: 1-60044-275-7
 1. Tribology--Juvenile literature. 2. Friction--Juvenile literature. 3. Lubrication and lubricants--Juvenile literature. 4. Building sites--Juvenile literature. I. Title. II. Series: Whitehouse, Patricia, 1958- Construction forces.

Printed in the USA

CG/CG

Rourke Publishing

www.rourkepublishing.com – sales@rourkepublishing.com
Post Office Box 3328, Vero Beach, FL 32964
1-800-394-7055

Tabla de contenido / Table of Contents

Local de construcción / Construction Site	4
Cosas que se pegan y que se deslizan / Things That Stick and Slide	6
La fricción / Friction	8
Cuando el deslizar es bueno / When Sliding is Good	10
Cuando el deslizer es malo / When Sliding is Bad	12
Cuando el agarre es bueno / When Sticking is Good	14
Cuando el agarre es malo / When Sticking is Bad	16
Cambiando la fricción / Changing Friction	18
Los frenos y la fricción / Brakes and Friction	20
¡Inténtalo! / Try It!	22
Glosario / Glossary	23
Índice / Index	24

Local de construcción
Construction Site

Esto es un **local de construcción**. Personas y **máquinas** trabajan aquí.

This is a **construction site**. People and **machines** work here.

Aquí, algunas cosas se deslizan. Otras cosas se pegan. Debido a la fricción, cosas se pegan y se deslizan.

Some things slip here. Some things stick. Sticking and slipping happen because of friction.

Cosas que se pegan y que se deslizan
Things That Stick and Slide

Algunas cosas en un local de construcción se deslizan. Los rollos de pintura se deslizan por las paredes.

Some things at a construction site slide or glide. Paint rollers glide on the walls.

Algunas cosas en un local de construcción se pegan o agarran. Los guantes de trabajo ayudan a agarrar los mangos de **herramientas**.

Some things at a construction site stick or grip. Work gloves help to grip **tool** handles.

La fricción
Friction

La fricción es una **fuerza.** La fricción hace posible que no se mueva la tierra.

Friction is a **force**. It keeps the dirt from moving.

Algunos trabajos necesitan mucha fricción. La fricción ayuda a los trabajadores a quedarse en el techo.

Some jobs need a lot of friction. Friction helps the workers stay on the roof.

Cuando el deslizar es bueno
When Sliding is Good

Una pequeña cantidad de fricción sostiene el cable en su lugar. El cable se desliza hacia arriba y hacia abajo en la grúa.

A little friction holds the cable in place. It can slide up and down the crane.

El tanque de la mezcladora da vueltas. No hay mucha fricción para detenerlo.

The tank on the concrete mixer spins around. There is not much friction to stop the spinning.

Cuando el deslizar es malo
When Sliding is Bad

Las ruedas del camión resbalan en el lodo. No pueden agarrarse. No hay suficiente fricción.

The truck tires spin in the mud. It cannot grip. There is not enough friction.

Esta carretera está cubierta de nieve. Las ruedas resbalarán. Las calles nevadas no tienen suficiente fricción.

This road has snow on it. Tires will slip. Snowy roads do not have much friction.

Cuando el agarre es bueno
When Sticking is Good

El uso de cadenas le da más fricción a las ruedas. Máquinas que operan en el lodo o en la nieve necesitan más fricción.

Using tire chains gives tires more friction. Machines working in mud or snow need more friction.

Los peldaños de esta escalera son ásperos. Los trabajadores no resbalarán. Esto es un buen lugar para la fricción.

The steps on the ladder are rough. Workers will not slip. This is a good place for friction.

Cuando el agarre es malo
When Sticking is Bad

Las piezas de este **motor** frotan unas contra otras. La fricción puede hacer que las piezas se pongan muy calientes. Entonces, el motor no funcionará.

Parts of this **engine** rub together. Friction might make the parts get too hot. Then the engine will not work.

Los tubos en el andamio están pegados. Frotan unas contra otras. Hay demasiada fricción.

The pipes on the scaffold are stuck. They rub together. There is too much friction.

Cambiando la fricción
Changing Friction

El añadir **aceite** reduc la fricción. Personas ponen aceite a los motores. Esto permite que las partes del motor se deslicen.

Adding **oil** makes less friction. People put oil into engines. Then the engine parts slide.

Un camión le hecha arena a una carretera helada. Las ruedas agarran la arena. Ahora hay más fricción.

A truck adds sand to an icy road. The tire grips the sand. Now there is more friction.

Los frenos y la fricción
Brakes and Friction

Todos los camiones usan frenos para detenerse. Los frenos usan la fricción para funcionar.

All trucks use brakes to stop. Brakes use friction to work.

Los choferes pisan el pedal del freno. Al pisar el freno, se crea fricción.

Drivers step on the brake pedal. Stepping on the brakes adds friction.

¡Inténtalo!
Try It!

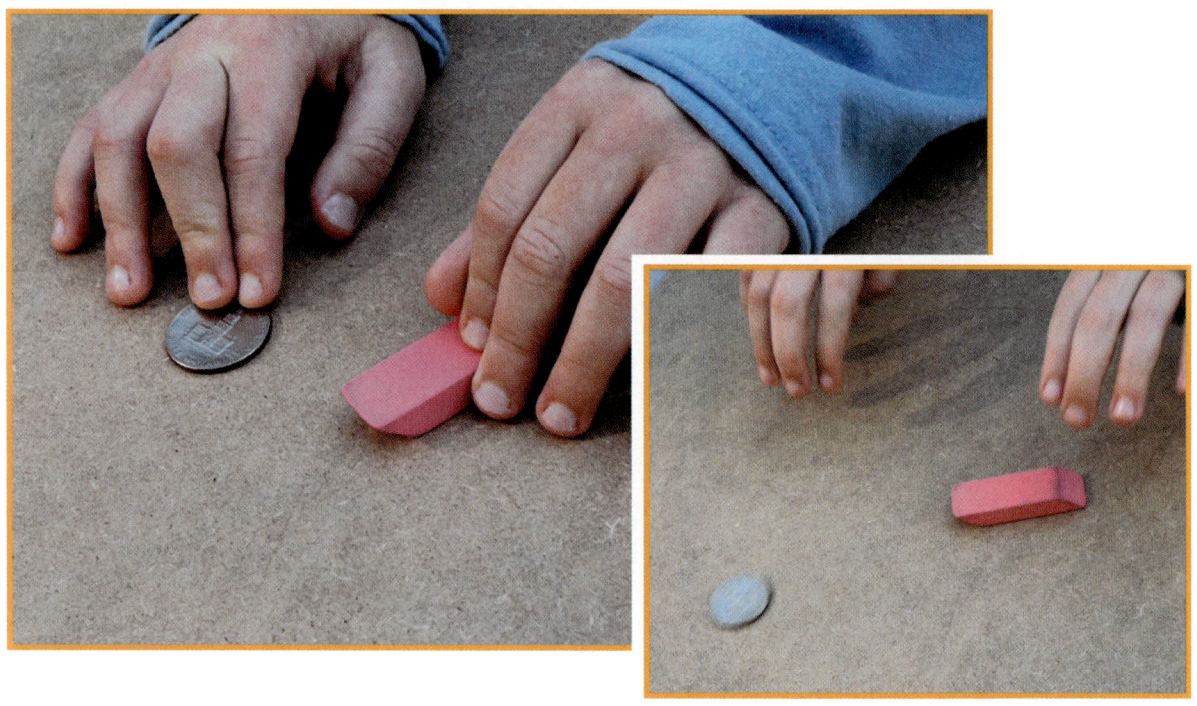

Tú puedes hacer una carrera usando la fricción. Pon una moneda y una goma de borrar en una superficie inclinada. Suéltalas para ver lo que hace la fricción.

You can have a friction race. Put a coin and eraser on a slide. Let go to see what friction will do.

GLOSARIO / GLOSSARY

local de construcción: lugar donde albañiles construyen algo
construction site (kuhn STRUHKT shun SITE): a place where workers build

motor: parte de un auto o camión que le permite moverse
engine (EN jun): part of a car or truck that makes it move

fuerza: el empujar o halar
force (FORSS): a push or a pull

aceite: líquido grasoso que hace que las cosas resbalen
oil (OIL): liquid that makes things slippery

máquina: algo que usa energía para ayudar a las personas a trabajar
machine (muh SHEEN): something that uses energy to help people work

herramienta: algo que se usa para hacer trabajo
tool (TOOL): something used to do work

ÍNDICE / INDEX

motor / engine   16, 18
agarre / grip   7, 12, 14, 16, 19
hielo / ice   19
frotar / rub   16, 17
resbalar / slip   5, 13, 15

OTROS LIBROS SOBRE EL TEMA / FURTHER READING
Parker, Steve. *Forces and Motion.* Chelsea House Publishers, 2005.
Trumbauer, Lisa. *What is Friction?* Children's Press, New York: 2004.
Whyman, Kathryn. *Forces in Action.* Stargazer Books, 2005.

PÁGUBAS WEB RECOMENDADAS / WEBSITES TO VISIT
http://www.bbc.co.uk/schools/revisewise/science/physical/12b_act.shtml
http://science.howstuffworks.com/engineering-channel.htm
http://www.bobthebuilder.com/usa/index.html

NOTAS SOBRE EL AUTOR / ABOUT THE AUTHOR
Patty Whitehouse has been a teacher for 17 years. She is currently a Lead Science teacher in Chicago, where she lives with her husband and two teenage children. She is the author of more than 100 books about science for children.